Copyrights

Copyright 2022 by Good News Meditations Kids - All rights reserved

This book or parts thereof may not be reproduced in any form, stored in any retrieval system, or transmitted in any form by any means—electronic, mechanical, photocopy, recording, or otherwise—without prior written permission of the copyright holder.

www.gnmkids.com

This book belongs to:

_____

**Macy's friends have come today!
In her backyard, they laugh and play.**

The sun has gone down. Look at the sky.
Time to go home – Goodbye! Goodbye!
She tells her friends, "Please come again!"
Now Macy is tired. It's time to go in.

There on the table, what does she see?
A slice of cake! Yippee! Yippee!
She gobbles it up. "Mmmmm! That's **good**" –
But Macy forgot to ask if she **could**!

"Where is the cake? Where did it go?"
Mother asks. "Does anyone know?"
"Not me!" says Macy, but that's not true;
Macy has lied, a wrong thing to do!

**Mother is sad, for it was her plan
To give the cake to Aunt Mary Ann,
Who's sick in bed, so mom thought she'd take
To cheer her up, a slice of cake.**

Every night, before going to bed
Daddy tells stories to fill Macy's head
With happy thoughts that help her to rest –
Macy thinks stories of Jesus are best!

He tells her a story of Jesus, Our King,
Our Savior, and Ruler of **Everything**,
Who told the people, – "I'm God's Own Son." –
Some people believed, but not **everyone**.

"We don't believe you!" some folks declared,
But Jesus stood strong. He was not scared,
Though they wanted to hurt Him – How unkind!
Their hearts were hard; they'd made up their mind.
But Jesus was truthful, no matter what,
For Jesus can't lie. No, He cannot!

Macy remembers the lie that she had
Told to her Mother, and that makes her sad.
"I wasn't like Jesus. I told a lie,"
She tells her Daddy then starts to cry.

"I ate the cake, but then I denied it.
I told a lie, in hopes I could hide it!
I let Mommy down. I hurt her heart.
I want to do better; it's time I start!"

"I'll always be truthful unlike before.
Like Jesus," says Macy, "I'll lie no more!"
Daddy says, "Macy, I'm so proud of you.
Telling the truth is the right thing to do."

One thing more, now that she has begun
Macy's aware which still must be done.
She confesses to Mother, "I don't know why,
But I ate the cake and then told a lie.
To make it right, do you think I can
Bake a new cake for Aunt Mary Ann?"

Mother says, "Macy, I've been concerned.
I knew you'd lied, but I'm glad you've learned.
Telling the truth was a hard thing to do.
You are forgiven, and I'm proud of you!"

The family then bows their heads to pray:
"Dear God, please help Macy every day.
Be by her side in all that she does,
So she can be truthful like Jesus was.
    --- In His Name, Amen"

Wherefore putting away lying, speak every man truth with his neighbour: for we are members one of another.

Ephesians 4v25 KJV

Author's note:

Thank you so much for reading this book.
If you enjoyed this book, we would love it
if you could leave a review or recommend it
to a friend.

If you want the coloring book or the audiobook for free please visit:

gnmkids.com

Thank you for your support!
Please checkout our other books

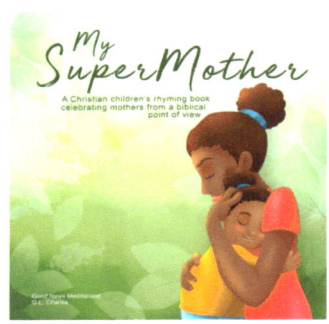

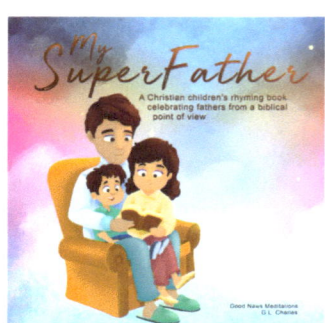

gnmkids.com